LEAD WITH NO FEAR
WORKBOOK

Foreword by Bob Burg, Co-Author of *The Go-Giver*

Your 90-day leader shift from worry, insecurity, and self-doubt to inspiration, clarity, and confidence.

Designed Action Plan for Leaders and Teams

Steve Gutzler & Mike Acker

COPYRIGHT ©2020,
MIKE ACKER AND STEVE GUTZLER

All rights reserved. No part of this publication may be reproduced, distributed, or transmitted in any form or by any means, including, photocopying, recording, or other electronic or mechanical methods, without the prior written permission of the publisher, except in the case of brief quotations embodied in reviews and certain other non-commercial uses permitted by copyright law.

Some names and identifying details have been changed to protect the privacy of individuals.

ISBN: 978-1-17349756-6-6

To contact, please email: contact@nofearworkshop.com

"You are now at a crossroads. Forget your past. Who are you now? Don't think about who you have been. Who have you decided to become? Make it carefully. Make it powerfully. Then act upon it."
- Anthony Robbins

"Give yourself permission to begin again. One, three-degree shift over the course of 90-days can place you in a whole new direction with new exciting results."
- Steve Gutzler and Mike Acker

THE GUIDING PRINCIPLE: YOUR 3° SHIFT

When Captain JJ Cummings, Commander of the World's Largest Aircraft Carrier, commanded the USS Gerald R. Ford to shift direction by three degree to the right, very few of the 4,550 crew members took notice. Ninety days later, however, when the 1,092-foot-long carrier arrived, crew members realized they'd traveled to a totally different continent.

Leadership, in many respects, is like strategically shifting your course, often every ninety days, not in big dramatic announcements or bold claims, but subtle 3° choices and intentional shifts.

In observing and working with hundreds of leaders and organizations in the fields of technology, medicine, government agencies, and in the service industry over a combined fifty years, we've uncovered seven critical shifts impactful leaders make to move from a fear-based default leadership style to one that exudes positive influence, sustainable impact, and inspires others to greatness by how they live and lead daily.

We invite you to make subtle changes by illuminating, motivating, and guiding you through the seven strategies. Initially, you may feel that you are not making tremendous headway, but when you begin to employ the 3° shift, you will end up in a completely different destination than where you began.

ME TO WE LEADER SHIFT

Commander JJ Cummings has thought a lot about his 'captainness' and leadership. On or off the ship, inside and outside the Navy, there are good and bad leaders. There are leaders who instill fear and leaders who inspire confidence. Cummings says, "Poor leaders are focused on their next job or promotion rather than thinking about this as their last job."

We've all seen poor leadership in action. It's short-sighted and insecure, a self-centeredness driven by fear and scarcity. In contrast, the centered and influential leaders serve selflessly. They make sacrifices and drive human potential to soaring new heights in business and non-profit work.

When Cummings attends Change of Command Ceremonies, he plays a mental game: How many times does the commander say, "I or me" instead of "we, our, or us"? Often, the ratio isn't good.

Your leader shifts are not just about you. Simply put, leadership is influence; and you have a shipload of people you are impacting through your daily decisions. Although these shifts are not just about you, they do start with you. As you begin to shift, you will be positively affecting your life and the individual lives of those around you.

"Leader shifts are a 'we' thing that start as a 'me' thing."

Foreword by Bob Burg, bestselling coauthor of The Go-Giver

The legendary leadership authority, John Maxwell has often said that "everything rises and falls on leadership."

It seems to me a very accurate statement. Nothing truly productive ever happens until someone casts a vision for that idea, and then they or someone else leads the way in bringing that idea to fruition.

In any business, large or small, its entire culture begins with its leadership, and the quality and character of that leadership filters throughout its ranks—whether positive, inspiring, and benevolent or negative, stifling, and malevolent.

The latter, unfortunately, is a good deal more common, perhaps in part because the former takes a good deal more work.

And here is the interesting part: for a leader to effectively provide that kind of powerfully positive leadership, they must first be able to lead themselves.

This takes awareness, acceptance, and a focused, concentrated effort.

If you are that leader, then this is where Steve Gutzler and Mike Acker come into your life.

There is a reason these two are regarded as premier leadership coaches. Steve and Mike have been in the trenches and know what it takes to lead. What's more, they know how to communicate their message in a clear, understandable, and actionable way that will allow you to make extraordinary gains, and do so relatively quickly.

In fact, the proven wisdom they share in this fantastic book has proven to help leaders make that all-important shift in just 90 days. Follow their guidance and watch yourself grow in ways you may never have imagined. The result will be a dramatic improvement in your leadership and effectiveness, more respect from those you lead, and the personal sense of happiness that flows from living and leading in a way congruent with your values.

In our current times, especially, the ability to lead in a way that inspires, influences, and ultimate impacts others will make you of infinitely more value to any group or organization. Their book will make an enormously positive difference for you, for those you lead, and for all those whose lives will eventually be touched in the process.

Steve and Mike will help you get there!

INTRODUCTION

What is the one thing all successful leaders have in common?

For over a collective forty years, we have asked ourselves and the numerous leaders and global teams we've worked with this question. Leadership, after all, drives nearly all great causes, accomplishments, and results.

In leadership development, great qualities come to mind: leaders are inspired, focused, visionary, innovative, impactful, brilliant, and sometimes a little eccentric. Ask a hundred people and you'll get a hundred answers.

In reality, leadership is not a one-cut diamond, it's multi-dimensional and multi-faceted.

The truth is, you'll never find a successful leader who drifted into success. They were intentional and set out a navigated course. At times, in fact at critical times, they had the courage to make some strategic shifts in direction. These were not quantum leaps or unrealistic attempts to radically change who they are, but rather 3° shifts in seven strategic areas of leadership. Over the course of 30, 60, or 90-days, these shifts had an extraordinary effect on their leadership influence, impact, and inspiration.

SEVEN SHIFTS TOWARD YOUR 3° DIFFERENCE

1. Shift from Victim to Leader
2. Shift from Unaware to Aware
3. Shift from from Black & White to HD
4. Shift from Insecure to Confident
5. Shift from Activity to Accomplishment
6. Shift from Smart to Smart & Healthy
7. Shift from Fast to Finishing

"I am not what happened to me,
I am what I choose to become."
— **Carl Jung**

"A smooth sea never made a skilled sailor."
— **Frank D. Roosevelt**

This workbook is designed to be a complement to our book, Lead With No Fear. We believe all significant change begins with identifying a key shift and then courageously making 3° actions.

Take the time to utilize our action sheets and set some new inspiring SMART (Specific, Measurable, Attainable, Relevant, and Time-bound) goals. We promise you will begin to shift over the next ninety days, you will see massive results in your leadership, inspiration, and confidence.

- You will learn to replace small thoughts and increase a powerful new inner dialogue.
- You will learn to replace worry, stress, and fear with newfound courage and confidence
- You will make lasting impact and create relationships that are loyal and meaningful
- You will inspire others to greatness with a servant leadership that sets you apart, a true lasting legacy

Whether you use our Lead With No Fear Workbook with a team or by yourself, answer each question honestly and set goals that drive your three-degree shifts.

May you lead with no fear!

Let's get started!

CHAPTER 1
SHIFT FROM VICTIM TO LEADER

"The victim is so caught up in small thinking and their victim story that they cannot listen to 'what's possible' or see their own behavior is creating the results of their lives."
- **Steve Gutzler and Mike Acker**

"Instill a mentality of world-class. You've got to clean out your limited beliefs and your psychological sabotage."
- **Robin Sharma**

1. Reflect upon a time you were in the "doldrums" (drifting in circles), how did you receive a second wind?

2. Provide examples of a victim vocabulary. Include words and phrases that hold you back.

*"Victims talk about their problems;
leaders talk about their opportunities and solutions."*

3. Outline the powerful words and phrases of a leadership vocabulary.

4. List "eliminator words" that you will cut out of your inner dialogue and vocabulary:

*"Victims talk about what makes them tired;
leaders talk about what makes them inspired"*

CRITICAL EXAMPLES –
FEAR-BASED VS. LEAD WITH NO FEAR

Fear-Based Mentality:
- That step is way too aggressive
- We don't have the resources for that
- The deadline is too aggressive
- Last time we tried, we failed
- Our clients won't buy it
- It's a waste of energy
- We don't have the expertise
- Our team couldn't pull that off
- Things won't improve
- It's too bold
- We simply can't

Lead With No Fear Mentality:
- We have the solutions
- Problems fuel innovation
- We will change the landscape
- We are ready for the challenge
- Let's think big about what's possible
- Lead's lead the way
- Let's reallocate our resources
- Let's network and find great people/clients
- Let's take that calculated risk
- People will "love it" and purchase it
- Yes, we can!

5. Note intentional words and phrases you will think and speak going forward – this is essentially your updated leadership vocabulary:

COACHING CHALLENGE:

1. Decide the type of words you want to use as a leader and a team:

2. Defend yourself and team against the words that hold you back. What words hold you back?

3. Design three "self-talk" mantras. Rewrite them using first-person pronouns and speak them daily below:

4. Set one SMART (Specific, Measurable, Attainable, Relevant, and Time-bound) goal for the next 30, 60, and 90-days.

- 30-Day SMART goal:

- 60-day SMART goal:

- 90-day SMART goal:

CHAPTER 2
SHIFT FROM UNAWARE TO SELF-AWARE

"We are dangerous when we are not self-aware and conscious of our responsibility for how we behave, think, and feel."
- **Marshall Goldberg**

"In a study of skills that distinguish star performers in every field from entry-level jobs to executives positions, the single most important factor was not IQ, advanced degrees, or technical experience, it was one's emotional intelligence of all the competencies required for excellence in performance in the job studies, 67% were emotional competencies."
- **Daniel Goleman**

Self-awareness is your ability as a personal leader to know and understand your strengths and primary gifts, as well as your weaknesses. It also is your ability to recognize the influence of your emotions on others and what you are transferring – your moods, attitudes, and emotions.

1. What are your two-primary strengths as a leader of influence, impact, and inspiration?

2. What are two potential liabilities (weaknesses) you need to be more aware of?

3. What are the three benefits of "seeking feedback" regarding your effectiveness as a leader?

4. Do you have a trusted peer, trusted advisor, or coach to gain greater self-awareness with? When can you seek feedback?

SELF-AWARENESS QUESTIONS ON VALUES AND LIFE GOALS

1. What does the ideal "you" look like as a leader of influence?

2. What is one big career aspiration that you have in the next 12-24 months?

3. What are your "top 3" career goals for the next 12-24 months?

4. What are one or two beliefs and behaviors that could hold you back from being your best?

5. What are your top 5 values that guide your life and leadership?

SELF-AWARENESS QUESTIONS ON LEADERSHIP INFLUENCE

1. Why do you lead? What is your primary motivation?

2. What kind of leader do you want to be?

3. How will you grow in your self-awareness in the next 90-days?

4. How will you keep getting better over the next 90-days?

COACHING CHALLENGE:

1. How can you develop or improve your listening skills over the net 90-days?

2. How can you develop or improve your emotional self-management under stress over the next 90-days?

3. How can you develop your emotional influence of others (as a positive influencer) over the next 90-days?

4. Finally, set one SMART (Specific, Measurable, Attainable, Relevant, and Timebound) goal to grow your self-awareness over the next 30, 60, and 90 days.

- 30-Day SMART goal:

- 60-Day SMART goal:

- 90-Day SMART goal:

CHAPTER 3
SHIFT FROM BLACK AND WHITE TO HIGH-DEFINITION

"You can't do it unless you can imagine it."
- **George Lucas**

"Innovation distinguishes between a leader and a follower."
– **Steve Jobs**

"A leader has the vision and compelling conviction that a dream can be achieved. It is a man or woman who inspired the power and energy to get it done."
– **Steve Gutzler and Mike Acker**

What new opportunities do you see in the midst of turbulent change?

1. What new opportunities do you see in the midst of turbulent change for your **personal leadership**?

2. What new opportunities do you see in the midst of turbulent change for your **business**?

3. What new opportunities do you see in the midst of turbulent change for **new innovations to set you apart**?

Quick Restart for Vision

1. How can you lead yourself towards resetting a new vision?

2. What can you achieve in the next 90-days?

DISCOVER PLUS-ULTRA VISION

How can you shift you or your team to see "more beyond" what you see now?

1. What has blocked your imagination and ability to see "more beyond"?

2. What could happen to your business if you removed "small thinking"?

"Vision is a picture of the future which creates passion in the present."
– Steve Gutzler

"It's not just what you see, but what you don't see that determines your destination. Be brave to see "more beyond" where you are."
– Mike Acker

GAIN CLARITY: SHIFT FROM A BLACK & WHITE VISION TO HIGH-DEFINITION

1. What do you aspire to accomplish in the next 90-days,

- For your **business:**

- For your **leadership and your team**:

- For your **new clients**:

2. Why do you want it?

- What are the compelling reasons for your vision?

- What will the benefits and payoffs be?

- Who will benefit from your renewed vision?

COACHING CHALLENGE:

1. Who do you need to enlist in your day to day building of your vision?

2. What outside expert or specialist do you need?

3. Who will coach you to greatness and your full potential?

VISION ONE SHEET

As a personal leader (or as a team) write out your inspired vision that you'd like accomplished in the next 12-24 months. Be bold, be clear, and see the possibilities. Don't let comparison kill your vision. Don't let small thinking kill your vision. Don't let current challenges kill your vision.

"A dream is a compelling vision you see in your heart that's too big to accomplish without the help of others."
– Chris Hodges

CHAPTER 4
SHIFT FROM INSECURE TO CONFIDENT

"Each time we face our fears, we gain strength and confidence in the doing."
– **Theodore Roosevelt**

"If you hear a voice within you say, 'you cannot paint,' then by all means paint and that voice will be silenced."
– **Vincent Van Gough**

"Trust yourself. Create the kind of self that you will be happy to live with all your life. Make the most of yourself by fanning the tiny inner sparks of possibilities into flames of achievement."
– **Golda Meir**

What are the characteristics of an insecure leader?

What are the characteristics of a confident leader?

INSECURE VS. CONFIDENT

For each of the below questions, provide examples when answering.

1. How can you feel less threatened by the skills and success of others?

2. Provide an example of how you can embrace difficult conversations to improve yourself and
others' performance.

3. How can you welcome feedback and ways to increase your leadership influence, impact, and inspiration in the next 90-days?

YOUR 90-DAY SHIFT TO INCREASE CONFIDENCE

Discipline

Document one to two personal disciplines you will focus on to increase your confidence:

Personal Drive: Focus, Energy, and Extra Effort

Provide an example of how you can increase this in the next 90-days:

Determination

When do you need to display grit and the "bounce back factor"?

COACHING CHALLENGE OVER THE NEXT 90-DAYS

1. Where do you need to "push through" to gain greater confidence?

2. What is one limiting behavior that has held you back?

3. How will you eliminate that limiting behavior?

4. How will you display great, positive emotions in the next 90-days?

5. Document one big SMART (Specific, Measurable, Attainable, Relevant, and Timebound) goal for the next 90-days to display confidence in your leadership.

> "Confidence begins with living your values and believing in yourself while letting go of your past."
> **– Steve Gutzler and Mike Acker**

CHAPTER 5
SHIFT FROM ACTIVITY TO ACCOMPLISHMENT

"The key is not to prioritize what's on your schedule, but to schedule your priorities."
– **Stephen Covey**

"People who have a sense of peace that their priorities are in the right place also have a sense of humanity and a realistic view of life."
– **Patrick Lencioni**

"A leader that is thoughtful and centered can acutely concentrate on a few high priorities that will deliver the life of their greatest aspirations."
– **Steve Gutzler and Mike Acker**

MVPs (Most Valuable and Profitable)

1. List 8-10 of your MVP projects and work activities:

2. List 8-10 of your MVP business and work relationships:

3. Over the next 90-days, what can you…

- Delegate:

- Outsource:

- Eliminate:

4. What is your "things not to do" list?

5. What are your top 4 MVPs for the next 90-days (tasks, projects, and relationships that will provide the highest ROI, return on your investment)?

6. What would make the next 90-days a glowing success?

COACHING CHALLENGE:

Be conscious each day when selecting how to spend your time. Provide an example of a preferred day:

Avoid the subduction to drifting away from your focus. Provide an example of distraction and drifting:

Ask yourself, "What am I doing right now that will help me to achieve my desired must-haves?" and provide an example of a 3° shift you can make right now to ensure your success?

Reset from Activity to Accomplishment:

1. **Self-Leadership**: How will you best lead yourself to focus on MVP accomplishments?

2. **Lead Others**: How can you best lead your team to focus on high-value MVPs?

3. **Leave Your Device**: How can you reset boundaries to reduce the overuse of screen time and device distractions?

CHAPTER 6
SHIFT FROM SMART TO SMART AND HEALTHY

"The first wealth is health."
– **Ralph Waldo Emerson**

"Daring to set boundaries is about having the courage to love ourselves, even when we risk disappointing others."
– **Brené Brown**

"Happiness is not something you postpone for the future; it is something you design for the present."
– **John Rohn**

"Successful people are simply those with successful habits."
– **Brian Tracy**

According to Dr. Beth Frates, a Lifestyle Medicine Pioneer and Harvard Medical School faculty member, there are six critical areas to maintain for health and wellness:

1. Exercise
2. Nutrition
3. Sleep
4. Stress Management
5. Social Connections
6. Moderation or Elimination of Substances

Over the next 90-days, what two (2) categories would you like to enhance and focus on?

PHYSICAL BUCKET

40 EXTRAORDINARY REASONS LEADERS EXERCISE:

1. Lifts your mood and attitude
2. Improves your memory
3. Builds your self-concept
4. Keeps your brain fit
5. Keeps your body fit and strong
6. Boosts your mental health
7. Strengthens your immune system
8. Reduces stress and anxiety
9. Makes you feel happier
10. Has anti-aging effects
11. Improves skin tones and circulation
12. Improves quality of sleep
13. Helps joint function
14. Improves muscle strength
15. Sharpens memory
16. Lowers urges for addiction
17. Boosts creative memory
18. Helps focus
19. Boosts confidence
20. Improves body image
21. Improves eating habits
22. Increases longevity
23. Strengthens bones
24. Strengthens heart function
25. Improves posture
26. Prevents colds/illness
27. Improves cholesterol levels
28. Lowers blood pressure
29. Lowers risk of cancer
30. Lowers risk of diabetes
31. Fights dementia
32. Eases back pain
33. Reduces feelings of depression
34. Prevents muscle loss
35. Increases energy and stamina
36. Improves balance
37. Improves oxygen supply to cells
38. Improves personal presence
39. Improves quality of life
40. Increases joy in personal relationships

"Remember, health and fitness are the foundation of energy and energy is a leader's greatest asset."
— **Steve Gutzler and Mike Acker**

What two SMART goals will you set in the next 90-days for your physical bucket?

What are two 3° shifts you can make that are small but will compound in 90-days?

1. Identify two areas that drain your emotional health and wellness.

2. Provide one example where you can reduce or set new limits to technology and screen time.

3. List 8-10 activities, hobbies, or recreations that fill your emotional bucket.

4. What two (from the above list) can you apply and begin scheduling?

5. When will you start?

*Remember, you are not a **machine**, you are a **human being**.*

Soulful re-filling examples:
- Reconnecting to your purpose
- Times for solitude and reflection
- Slowing down for prayer and meditation
- Spiritual and inspiration readings
- Workshop communities or small group fellowship
- Journaling on soul-based reflections

How can you enrich your soulful bucket?

Now, set your new 90-day soulful SMART goal. Think along the lines of, "I plan to set a new practice in place and will commit to my soul nourishment."

1. What are the special family relationships you will commit to? Provide practical examples of how to connect.

2. Outline your key friendship and inner-circle relationships you will invest in:

SHIFT WITH THE BALANCE WHEEL

Identify the levels:

To shift from Smart to Smart AND Healthy, revisit the chapter on shifting from Smart to Smart AND Healthy and identify the levels of each bucket on a scale of 0 to 10 (on the wheel on the next page, the center is 0 and the edge is 10).

- Professional
- Physical
- Emotional
- Soulful
- Relational

Visualize your balance:

Mark the level on the wheel in each corresponding bucket, and draw a line across. You may choose to color the area up to the level you identified or scratch it in with a pen or pencil.

Check your overall health:

When all five parts of the wheel are complete, check the balance by considering how well your wheel would roll with current level (for example imagine a wheel with Productive - 9, Physical - 8, Emotional - 8, Soulful - 6, Relational - 2. Such a wheel would barely be able to role.)

- Professional
- Physical
- Emotional
- Soulful
- Relational

Use this visual to direct you to create a plan of action:

8 to 10: You are proficient to fill in that category. You'll want to keep watch for the "leaky bucket" syndrome and ensure that this bucket is maintained.

5 to 7: Although you are not fully drained, you realize you are lacking in this area. There is significant room for growth.

1 to 4: This is an urgent area needing your focus! Develop a plan to patch holes and fill this bucket. Why do you think your level is so low in this area?

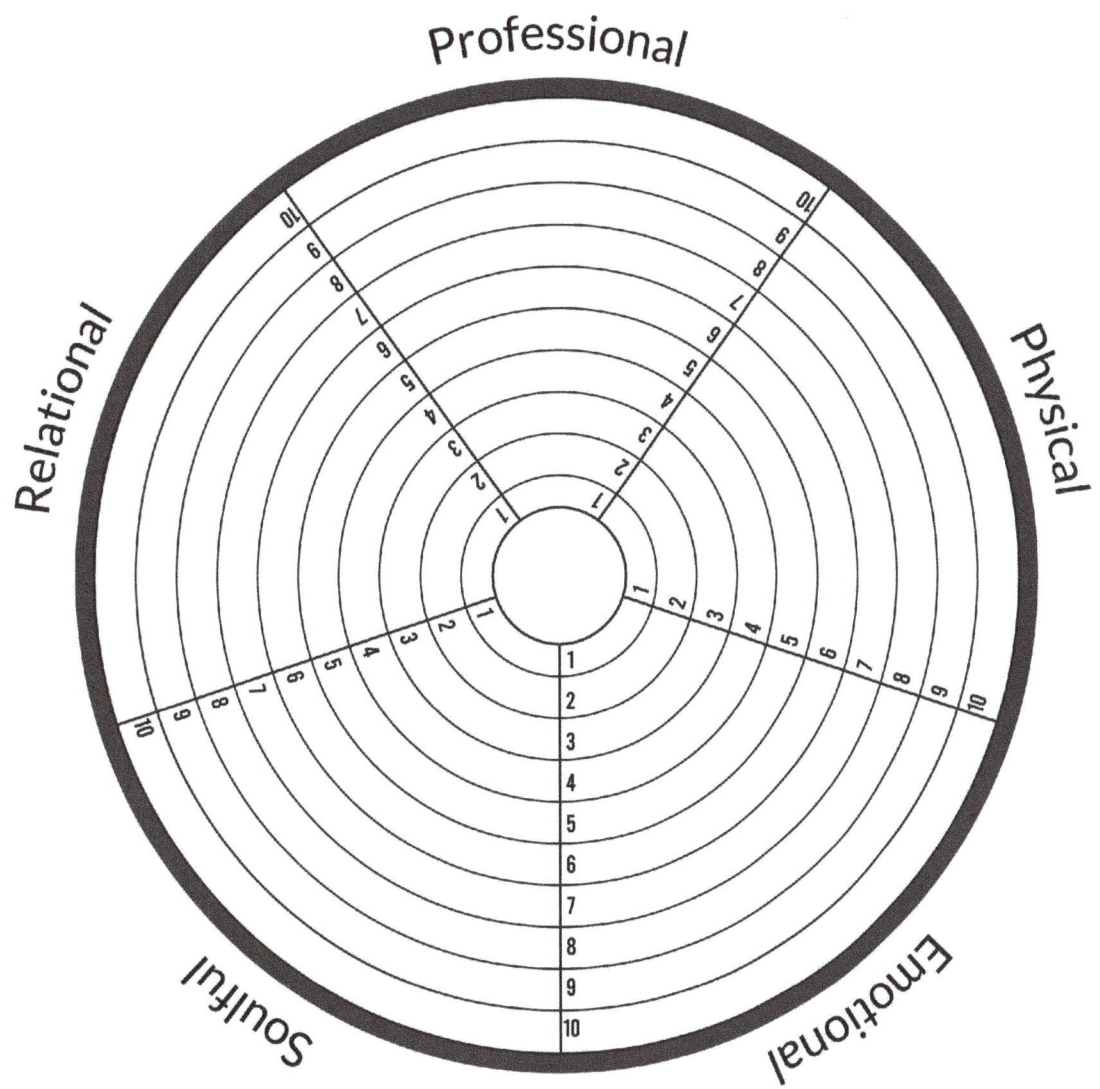

Which category from the Balance Wheel should you focus on first?

What is one step you can do today to patch up each area?

CHAPTER 7
SHIFT FROM FAST TO FINISHING

"Titles are granted but it's your behavior that earns you respect."
– **James M. Kouzes**

"Excellence is the gradual result of always striving to do better."
– **Pat Riley**

"The greatest leaders aren't necessarily the ones who do the greatest things. They are the ones who empower others to do great things."
– **John Maxwell**

1. Name three (3) leaders who you have admired and note the qualities that earned your respect.

2. How do you define "finishing well" as a personal leader?

Value Exercise:

1. Imagine someone you work for who appears to not value you. Choose something from this list that you could provide them with (circle all that apply).

Extra support	Personal sacrifice
Leads and referrals	Good advice
Encouragement	Empathy
Innovation	Tried and true techniques
Vision	Respect
Acceptance	Suggestions
Instructions to avoid costly mistakes	Protection
Basic Information	The benefit of the doubt
Passion	Feedback

2. Now imagine someone you work for whom you feel somewhat valued by. Using the list above, note what you would give them.

3. Next, imagine someone you work for whom you feel highly valued and empowered by, what would you give them? How does it differ and why?

4. What from the list are you receiving from others you lead and work with?

5. How can you show great appreciation and value to others?

6. How do you define servant leadership?

7. How do you lead from a place of ego and love?

8. What 3° shift can you make starting now to lead from love and service to others?

COACHING CHALLENGE SHIFTING FROM FAST TO FINISHING WELL:

1. How can you shift in the next 90-days to a more genuine connection between those you serve?

2. How can you shift to meeting the needs of your team and show a deeper level of respect?

3. We will all be remembered for something. The question is what. What will others say about you when you are no longer around? What shift can you make now to ensure a lasting legacy of purpose?

4. Note five (5) words to describe your leadership with no fear.

90-DAY ACTION PLAN

THE SEVEN SHIFTS:

1. Victim to Leader
2. Unaware to Aware
3. From Black & White to HD
4. Insecure to Confident
5. Activity to Accomplishment
6. Smart to Smart & Healthy
7. Fast to Finishing

YOUR DAILY/WEEKLY ACTION PLAN:

1. Select one (1) shift to focus on this day and/or week:

2. List the MVP (Most Valuable and Profitable) accomplishments you must complete this week:

3. List projects to work on one step at a time (at a minimum) each day:

4. Note one fear to identify and eliminate this week:

YOUR DAILY/WEEKLY ACTION PLAN:

5. List words, affirmations, and leadership vocabulary you will speak this week:

6. Outline one SMART (Specific, Measurable, Attainable, Relevant, and Timebound) goal for your professional career this week:

YOUR 90-DAY (QUARTERLY) ACTION PLAN:

1. Select three (3) shifts to focus on this quarter:

2. Outline three (3) MVP accomplishments you'd like to accomplish this quarter:

3. What are your top five (5) projects for this quarter?

4. Reflect to identify two (2) fears you'd like to eliminate this quarter:

YOUR 90-DAY (QUARTERLY) ACTION PLAN:

5. What words of affirmation and leadership vocabulary would you like to speak this quarter?

6. Select three (3) SMART goals to set professionally this quarter:

YOUR ANNUAL REFLECT AND REVIEW:

1. What is your purpose and vision for your life and leadership?

2. What is your vision for your business or role at work?

3. What are your top five (5) values for life and leadership?

4. Outline your top five (5) personal goals for this year:

5. Select and note three (3) top shifts for this year:

YOUR ANNUAL REFLECT AND REVIEW:

6. What new developing skills would you like to focus on this year?

7. What are your top 20 MVP contacts to make this year?

PRINTABLE REFLECT AND REVIEW RESOURCES ARE AVAILABLE ONLINE:

https://nofearworkshop.com/daily

https://nofearworkshop.com/quarterly

https://nofearworkshop.com/annual

THE BELOW SPACE IS FOR YOUR NOTES, IDEAS, AND INSPIRATION (MENTORS AND COACHING).

"Whatever the mind can conceive and believe, it can achieve."
- **Napoleon Hill, Bestselling author of Think and Grow Rich (1883 – 1970)**

LEAD WITH NO FEAR
LEADERSHIP ASSESSMENT

On the next two (2) pages, use the scoring scale below to rate yourself on each line item. At the conclusion of this assessment, you will add up all scores to determine your Lead With No Fear Leadership rating.

SCORING SCALE:
0 = Never
1 = Seldom
2 = Sometimes
3 = Usually
4 = Always

LEADERSHIP ASSESSMENT

Shift from Victim to Leader

1. I have identified self-talk derailers:

2. I am intentional with a leadership vocabulary:

3. I have eliminated fear-based words:

4. I speak like a leader and empower others:

5. I am aware of my strengths and gifts:

6. I am aware of weakness and strive for improvement:

7. I recognize my mood, attitudes, and emotions are contagious:

8. I am open to 360° feedback:

9. I have a clear and vivid vision:

10. I take the time to set specific goals for my vision:

11. I believe there is "more beyond" this vision:

12. I take time to vision-cast for my team and colleagues:

13. I know my insecure leadership defaults:

LEADERSHIP ASSESSMENT

14. I celebrate the win and successes of others:

15. I am centered on my purpose:

16. I focus on my MVPs (most valuable and profitable):

17. I time-block around high-value work:

18. I eliminate time-wasters:

19. I fill my physical bucket daily/weekly:

20. I fill my emotional bucket daily/weekly:

21. I fill my soulful bucket daily/weekly:

22. I fill my relational bucket daily/weekly:

23. I lead from a servant leadership style:

24. I connect genuinely with my team:

25. I lead with a goal of a lasting legacy:

SCORING SCALE

90 - 100: Great leader without fear
80 - 89: Good leader manages fear well
70 - 79: Emerging leader aware of fear and overcoming
60 – 69: Bursting with potential looking to overcome fear
Below 60: Needs growth and accountability for growth

LEADERSHIP ASSESSMENT SMART GOAL

Set one (1) SMART (Specific, Measurable, Attainable, Relevant, and Timebound) goal for the next 90-days to improve your assessment score.

90-DAY GOALS

Use the boxes below to set your 90-day goal for each of the seven shifts.

Shifting from victim to leader is:

Shifting from unaware to self-aware is:

Shifting from black & white to high-definition is:

Shifting from insecure to secure is:

90-DAY GOALS

Shifting from activity to accomplishment is:

Shifting from smart to smart AND healthy is:

Shifting from fast to finishing is:

CONCLUSION

We both have a small "post-it note" on our desks. It reads:
1440.

1440. That's how many minutes we get, each and every day, to lead our lives and leave our legacies. It's a simple reminder to invest time in meaningful work and purposeful relationships.

We've found we need to focus on our energy. That's the one thing we can influence most.

In The Power of Full Engagement, authors Jim Loehr and Tony Schwartz write: "Energy, not time, is the fundamental currency of high performance." They go on to explain, "The ultimate measure of our lives is not how much time we spend on the planet, but rather how much energy we invest in the time we have."

Their premise is simple: Performance, health, and happiness are improved through the skillful management of energy. The number of hours in a day is fixed, but the quantity and quality of energy can be cultivated. It is our most precious resource.

The more we take responsibility for the energy we bring to the world, the more empowered and productive we become. The more we blame others or external circumstances, the more negative and compromised our energy is going to be.

People who strive boldly and reach their potential do not sit back and wait for things to happen. They identify limiting beliefs and fears that hold them back. They expose those beliefs to a new paradigm of energy and focus. They reverse limiting behaviors that erode their goals and dreams.

They shift.

High performing leaders start by working on themselves.

High-performing leaders also start one step at a time.

JUST 3°

Transformation is possible. With 3° shifts, small, incremental, and intentional actions, you will achieve real and lasting results.

First Shift: From Victim to Leader
Rid yourself of a victim mindset, victim self-talk, and victim vocabulary.

Second Shift: From Unaware to Self-aware
Discover your blind spots and understand how others perceive your leadership.

Third Shift: From Black and White to High-Definition
Clarify your personal vision for life and professional vision for leadership.

Fourth Shift: From Insecure to Confident
Move from dwelling on your deficiencies to focusing on what you can give.

Fifth Shift: From Activity to Accomplishment
Focus on the most valuable and profitable priorities, not checking things off a list for instant gratification.

Sixth Shift: From Smart to Smart AND Healthy
Discover how balance in life benefits work, relationships, health, and everything else.

Seventh Shift: From Fast to Finishing
Dream about how to build your legacy, not just your resume. These seven shifts, combined with consistent and positive action, will create the lasting legacy you desire and lead you to your desired destination.

"MIRACULOUS" DESTINATIONS

MIKE: Rachel Richards, the author of a bestselling book on financial management, came to me as a communication client. Agents had begun to reach out to her for keynotes, and she needed help preparing for media appearances.

It was while I coached Rachel that I felt inspired to write my first book, Speak With No Fear. I asked her for advice about writing. "Do it one day at a time," she replied.

Every day, Rachel worked on her book. When she completed her first book, she worked on promoting it every day. Then she began to work on her second book. For two years, she worked on Passive Income, Aggressive Retirement. She published her book in 2019.

Ultimately, Rachel Richards retired at the age of 27.

When she first started writing at 23, she didn't know what exact destination she would end up at. She just knew that she needed to make a shift, one day at a time.

What shift will you begin to make one day at a time?

"MIRACULOUS" DECISIONS

Kevin James stars as Albert Brennaman in the movie Hitch. Kevin's character, Albert, is desperately in love with Allegra Cole, a beautiful woman who works with his financial firm for her financial investment. To Allegra, Albert is just another man in a black suit who manages her vast wealth. Albert would have continued going by unnoticed had he not decided to do something differently.

Albert seeks out a coach in Will Smith's character, Alex "Hitch" Hitchens. In the movie, Hitch leads Albert to do something different: Hitch challenges Albert to stand out, overcome his fears, and take a risk.

And so Albert Brennaman takes action, faces his fears, and boldly speaks out. He confronts his boss, challenges Allegra to take action, and quits his job.

No, we're not saying you need to quit your job. We're saying:

You need an Albert Brennaman moment!

After all, if you always do what you've always done, you will get what you've always got.

And we know that if you've picked up this book and read till this point, the final section, you have what it takes to make those 3° shifts, create a legacy that means something, and lead with no fear.

You've got it in you.

"MIRACULOUS" DECISIONS

Kevin James stars as Albert Brennaman in the movie Hitch. Kevin's character, Albert, is desperately in love with Allegra Cole, a beautiful woman who works with his financial firm for her financial investment. To Allegra, Albert is just another man in a black suit who manages her vast wealth. Albert would have continued going by unnoticed had he not decided to do something differently.

Albert seeks out a coach in Will Smith's character, Alex "Hitch" Hitchens. In the movie, Hitch leads Albert to do something different: Hitch challenges Albert to stand out, overcome his fears, and take a risk.

And so Albert Brennaman takes action, faces his fears, and boldly speaks out. He confronts his boss, challenges Allegra to take action, and quits his job.

No, we're not saying you need to quit your job. We're saying:

You need an Albert Brennaman moment!

After all, if you always do what you've always done, you will get what you've always got.

And we know that if you've picked up this book and read till this point, the final section, you have what it takes to make those 3° shifts, create a legacy that means something, and lead with no fear.

You've got it in you.

"MIRACULOUS" DESTINATIONS

MIKE: Rachel Richards, the author of a bestselling book on financial management, came to me as a communication client. Agents had begun to reach out to her for keynotes, and she needed help preparing for media appearances.

It was while I coached Rachel that I felt inspired to write my first book, Speak With No Fear. I asked her for advice about writing. "Do it one day at a time," she replied.

Every day, Rachel worked on her book. When she completed her first book, she worked on promoting it every day. Then she began to work on her second book. For two years, she worked on Passive Income, Aggressive Retirement. She published her book in 2019.

Ultimately, Rachel Richards retired at the age of 27.

When she first started writing at 23, she didn't know what exact destination she would end up at. She just knew that she needed to make a shift, one day at a time.

What shift will you begin to make one day at a time?

MAKE SURE TO A-C-T

We titled this book: Lead With No Fear: Your 90-day Leadership Shift from Worry, Insecurity, and Self-doubt to Inspiration, Clarity, and Confidence.

In order for you to maximize this claim, you must A-C-T:
Apply, Change, Transfer.

PARTICIPATE IN YOUR OWN RESCUE

STEVE: During my transforming experience of rafting and kayaking with burn survivors, we traveled many miles, navigating calm waters and turbulent whitewater rapids. During the orientation, the guides warned that there were "no joke" serious rapids ahead, and that we would flip our kayaks from time to time.

The instructions were clear: "As soon as you flip out of your kayak, sit up in the high, point your feet downstream, use your legs to push off any upcoming rocks, and we will throw you a line with a handle on it. Your responsibility is to grab that line and pull yourself toward us. You will need to participate in your own rescue!"

Rescue could not be passive. We had to be active, aggressive, and we had to participate.

As authors and leadership coaches, we've done our best to provide actionable points to lead with no fear. Now, it's time for you to participate and actively engage.

A—APPLICATION

Over the next 90 days, methodically focus on these seven strategies. Apply a 3° shift and set an actionable goal for the next 90 days.

We make our habits and our habits make us.

Use the content and questions from the chapters to develop your own life motto, mission, or vision.

You may gain inspiration by searching online or by studying sources such as The Four Agreements from David Forster:

1. Always do your best
2. Be impeccable with your words
3. Don't take things personally
4. Don't make assumptions

C–CHANGE

Courageously change limiting beliefs and behaviors in the next 90 days.

1. Can you identify a limiting belief that is holding you back? It could be:

- Lack of education
- Lack of experience or qualification
- Thinking you are too old
- A damaged self-concept from your youth
- A failure in your past seeded doubts and fears

It's time to take that limiting behavior and destroy it. Lean into what scares you, and it will get smaller and smaller. Soon, that once-debilitating belief will disappear.

2. Can you identify a limiting behavior that is holding you back? It could be:

- Procrastination
- Negative self-talk
- Eating poorly
- Getting distracted by news or social media

T–TRANSFER:

Share your shifts with others.

Don't be like a pond with just one source of water flowing in.
The healthiest lakes have a source flowing in and out. When you transfer knowledge and skills to others, you compound your success.

> "If your actions inspire others to dream more, learn more,
> do more, and become more, you are a leader."
> **— John Quincy Adams**

ACKNOWLEDGEMENTS

ACKNOWLEDGEMENTS BY STEVE

When my co-author, Mike Acker, and I sat at Wood's Coffee in Bellevue, Washington to discuss writing Lead With No Fear, I had no idea that COVID-19 would soon sweep through our world. I couldn't imagine that Kirkland, Washington, just 20-minutes from where I live outside of Seattle, would register as the national epicenter of the virus. Lead With No Fear guided us through this pandemic.

I first want to thank Mike for his dedication and devotion to this book. We cheered one another on to write with the belief that transformational change can occur in 3° shifts and within 90 days!

To my life partner, Julie, who leads fearlessly as my wife and mother to our three adult children, Jenna, Jayce, and Kyle, to their partners Kamran and Cherisse, and to my six grandchildren who keep us all young at heart with our frequent playground visits. You all are my "why" and my driving purpose to "inspire greatness in others."

A special thanks to my executive assistant, Jamie Pennington, who keeps my schedule, communicates with all my clients, arranges travel, orders my day, and typed every word of the chicken scratch I wrote, scanned, and sent her with this book project. You are only as good as your team, and I'm blessed beyond words to have Jamie, Michelle Joyce, Leeann Cannon, Gary Thompson, Brian Jeide, and Caleb Couch in my corner.

To my beloved parents, Tom and Carolyn Gutzler, who first modeled love and leadership to me, while teaching me the value of serving others, of generosity, and servant leadership. To my football coach, Don Matthew, who said, "You don't need to be a captain to be a leader." To my Pastor, Ron Mehl, who said, "Steve, you are a gifted communicator, you need to speak. "And to my God, who has chosen to use a flawed man to inspire greatness in others and lead with no fear!

Finally, to our readers: **We can lead with courage and clarity. Together, we can change the world!**

ACKNOWLEDGEMENTS BY MIKE

In January 2019, someone recommended Steve Gutzler to partner with me on a team event I was organizing. I needed to bring in a new voice, and Steve did an incredible job connecting with us, with incredible content, powerful stories, and a meaningful assignment.

After the event ended, Steve and I discovered that we had a family connection! His daughter and my sister had married brothers. With this extended family connection, similar lines of work, and a great personal connection, we decided to stay in contact. We reconnected just prior to the beginning of the coronavirus pandemic. As cafes closed, we decided to practice what we preach by finding opportunity in obstacles. Our Wood's Cafe idea would become this book. We hope to inspire others.

Working with Steve on this project has been incredible. We've pushed each other, encouraged each other, and brought out the best in each other. I want to thank Steve for taking this journey with me. I've become a better person, leader, coach, and author as a result. Thank you!

I heart-fully thank my wife every time I write a book, and I wish to thank her again! She allows me the time in the mornings and evenings to put on my Apple playlist and write. And write. And write. Thank you, Taylor, for your love, your work, and your patience!

A special thank you to Aimée Bruneau, our Lead Coach and Program Concierge at ADVANCE. She came to work with me at the perfect time. She provides incredible coaching, impeccable organization, and she has helped me get this ready to publish.

And thank **you** for entrusting us with your time and energy. **We hope that the stories, studies, and principles in this book inspire you to lead with motivation, clarity, and confidence!**

ABOUT STEVE

Steve Gutzler is an on-demand keynote speaker on emotional intelligence and transformational leadership. His principles and practices have inspired audiences around the country. He has partnered with and presented to major global brands and countless fortune-500 companies such as Microsoft, LinkedIn, Spotify, The Ritz Carlton, Seattle Seahawks, Boeing, Kraft Foods, and with federal agencies, law enforcement, hospitals, and technology startups.

He's a husband, father of three children, and grandfather to six grandchildren, who keep him young and a frequent playground visitor.

If you are interested in contacting Steve for a keynote program, team workshop, or online training:

email: Steve at contact@stevegutzler.com
website: www.SteveGutzler.com

You can also sign up for Steve's weekly leadership newsletter at:
www.SteveGutzler.com

ABOUT MIKE

Mike Acker is the CEO of ADVANCE where he leads his growing team on the mission to **turn people's potential into action** through workshops, communication programs, and executive coaching. His Speak and No Fear series of books inspire audiences to break through barriers to achieve new levels of success. ADVANCE has partnered with individuals and organizations close to home, and all over the world.

Mike enjoys rock-climbing, wake surfing, skiing, his church, building Legos with his son, and going on dates with his wife, Taylor. Mike believes in the power of prayer, in exercise, journaling, and leaning on his community in order to counter the stress of everyday life.

If you are interested in working with ADVANCE, please contact:
info@stepstoadvance.com

If you want to book Mike Acker for a speaking engagement, please contact:
mike.acker@stepstoadvance.com

To stay connected visit:
https://subscribe.stepstoadvance.com/me

BRING LEAD WITH NO FEAR TRAINING TO YOUR ORGANIZATION

DEVELOP Leadership
BUILD Your Team

OUR SERVICES

- Conference Keynotes
- Offsite Half or Full-Day Workshops
- Organizational Assessments and Resources
- 30-minute and 1-hour Virtual Trainings
- Coaching for Keynote Presentations
- Executive and Leadership coaching

EMAIL:
contact@nofearworkshop.com

BOOK STEVE GUTZLER

DISCOVER THE PROVEN PRINCIPLES AND PRACTICES THAT MAKE LEADERS GREAT AND TEAMS THRIVE

Steve Gutzler is an on-demand keynote speaker on emotional intelligence and transformational leadership. His principles and practices have inspired audiences around the nation.

He has partnered and presented with major global brands and countless fortune-500 companies such as Microsoft, LinkedIn, Spotify, The Ritz Carlton, Seattle Seahawks, Boeing, Kraft Foods, US Federal Agencies, Law Enforcement, Hospitals, and technology startups.

contact@stevegutzler.com

INSPIRE GREATNESS AND BRING OUT YOUR TEAMS BEST

Steve Gutzler is a uniquely different speaker. His authentic, inspiring style moves people to action. Steve has spent 25 years coaching, training, and working one on one with Fortune-500 companies and leading organizations such as Microsoft, Kraft Foods, LinkedIn, Spotify, The Ritz Carlton, Seattle Seahawks, Boeing, Federal US Agencies, Hospitals, and technology startups.

His keynote presentations teach today's leaders how to reach their full potential, build unstoppable inner confidence, and achieve sustainable success. He is a recognized expert of emotional intelligence and transformational leadership, and has delivered over 2,500 presentations. Steve's keynotes are a high-energy, motivational experience that will leave audiences inspired and moved to action.

If you are interested in booking Steve Gutzler for a keynote presentation, workshop, or online training, please contact **steve@stevegutzler.com** or visit **www.SteveGutzler.com**. You can also follow Steve on Twitter, Instagram, and Facebook.

"Steve Gutzler has been an irrefutable 'wow' during our Annual General Managers Conference, as well as our Leadership Team Advances. He has a unique way of bringing energy, authenticity, and actionable takeaways."

– Doug Dreher, CEO, The Hotel Group

BOOK MIKE ACKER

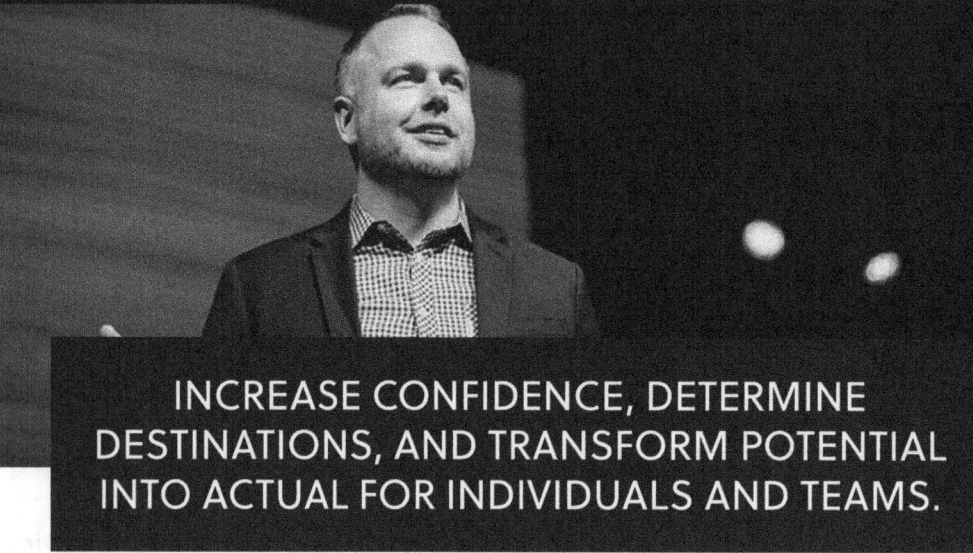

INCREASE CONFIDENCE, DETERMINE DESTINATIONS, AND TRANSFORM POTENTIAL INTO ACTUAL FOR INDIVIDUALS AND TEAMS.

Mike Acker is part of the John Maxwell Team. He is a certified leadership speaker, a gifted storyteller, and award winning Thumbtack Top Pro for event organizers. His presentations are prompted by his extensive personal leadership experience, his international upbringing and education, and his authorization to teach licenced material from leadership guru, John Maxwell.

In addition to speaking, he has trained many executives and teams in their communication and company leadership, including Adobe, Oracle and INOapps, Amazon, Microsoft, MLB, and Silicon Valley Startups. He has served as a speaker coach for TEDx presenters, orators, and politicians.

contact@mikeacker.com

If you are interested in inviting Mike Acker to speak for your event or coach your team email **contact@mikeacker.com**. He and his coaching team also blog on **www.stepstoadvance.com/blog** and can be found on LinkedIn, Twitter, and Facebook.

"I have had Mike speak at multiple functions of audiences from 20-500 people, and his ability to connect and motivate diverse groups of people is amazing! I would highly recommend Mike. Additionally, Mike has been a consistent encouragement in my own development. He gives good feedback and practical advice both on the stage and off."

– Micah Jaquay,
CEO, Praxis Technology

COPYRIGHT ©2020,
MIKE ACKER AND STEVE GUTZLER

All rights reserved. No part of this publication may be reproduced, distributed, or transmitted in any form or by any means, including photocopying, recording, or other electronic or mechanical methods, without the prior written permission of the publisher, except in the case of brief quotations embodied in reviews and certain other non-commercial uses permitted by copyright law.

Some names and identifying details have been changed to protect the privacy of individuals.

ISBN: 978-1-17349756-6-6

To contact, please email: contact@nofearworkshop.com

www.ingramcontent.com/pod-product-compliance
Lightning Source LLC
Chambersburg PA
CBHW081235080526
44587CB00022B/3943